Keeping House

fal

fal poetry

| Olga's Dreams | Victoria Field |
| Dear Shadows | DM Thomas |

Keeping House

Bill Mycock

fal

First edition 2004

ISBN 0-9544980-2-X

Cover design by Cassie Young

Cover image *Man Reading* (gouache and collage) by Bill Mycock

Acknowledgements

The North
Proof
Stray Dogs

Published by

Fal Publications
PO Box 74
Truro
TR1 1XS

www.falpublications.co.uk

Printed by

R. Booth Ltd
Antron Hill, Mabe,
Cornwall

To Hilda (1919-1992)
with affection for a sister and friend

Contents

Introduction

Many poems in this collection 'recount' memories. In the way that a memory recreates the past as we perceive it, a poem about the memory takes on a life of its own, parallel to the memory. Travelling, a foot in each track of memory and poem, has been exhilarating, a bit wild. And it is sometimes difficult to return to the 'pure' memories I began with. Other poems have 'appeared' from that dark corner of the mind where imagination brews its mysteries.

One particular memory is vivid:

Mid-morning, Michaelmas term, 1947. As he comes into the classroom, the English teacher puts down our pile of marked homework papers on the desk of the boy at the front. Taking the top one, he holds it in view to the class. Something like a gnat stings the lining of my bladder. "Some boy doesn't know who he is," he announces. "Whose is this?" Sluggishly my hand goes up. "You'd have got 10/10 with your name on it. As it is, nine."

Mr Torrance, whom we inexplicably knew as 'Neckie', stood monumental before us - his steel grey hair always neatly cut and combed, his master's gown over Harris tweed jacket and flannels - expounding in a baritone the joys of our rural ways of life and the idiosyncrasies of the English language. We had been looking at Thomas Hardy's Weathers and been asked to write our own versions of the poem. Mine began, 'This is the weather the hiker likes,/And so do I'. I had struggled hours under the Aladdin oil lamp at the supper table, my mother labouring as novice critic as I eventually soared 'over hedge, over ditch, eating brown bread rich'. That's as much as I remember of that first engagement in writing a poem - though it would be years before I felt compelled to continue.

In his long years of teaching, Neckie Torrance must have increased many boys' awareness and appreciation of good literature as well as of the everyday things around us and the pleasures of striving to further such interests. I remember, too, the headmistress of my village school where, warmed by coal fires in all three classrooms, we painted wartime posters to keep up morale during the early nineteen-forties. Such mentors are not always appreciated in their time. There are many others I've found influential in their wisdom or teaching, such as people I worked with in industry, adult education tutors and writers.

Perhaps I heeded because I couldn't make up my mind what it was I'd be happy to work at. I failed (or so it seems to me) my ancestors by breaking their long tradition of farming because I became besotted with flying. As a child, I saw the broken formations of Lancaster and Wellington bombers returning from day and night raids over Germany. I wasn't then aware of all the connotations of 'flying' and thought only of machines that took to the air. Dissuaded from joining the RAF on leaving school by my father's dislike of all things military, I found little excitement on taking up aeronautical engineering. The structural bits and pieces I learned to machine and rivet together, the thousands of tiny blue rivets I parted off in a sweltering machine shop, even designing minor parts and calculating their weights and their effect on the balance of an aeroplane, failed to inspire. Of course, it dawned on me that it was the observation and spirit of flying I enjoyed. Who can resist watching the fulmars ride the up-drafts on Cornwall's north cliffs? A creative work produced from direct observation, memory or a mysterious activity of the brain, seems to me to capture that spirit.

I hope the poems in this collection might succeed in manifesting that spirit. Poems, some say, come from the dark of the mind, almost unawares, though in my experience often needing encouragement and much work to finish. Henry Israel, a Cornwall-based drawing and painting tutor I greatly admire, would talk in his Life classes of a work being approached like the Zen archer looking away before he loosed the arrow. Something similar seems to happen in writing a poem: a looking away from oneself, the self becoming the poem. The flight of a poem may be a few minutes. Zing. There it is, conceived and on the page before you know it. Or it can take years, looked at now and then, shedding its encumbrances, gathering meat and eloquence in its trajectory until its beautiful whack into the target. Timeless.

Bill Mycock
January 2004
St Agnes
Cornwall

Keeping House, Jumember

Doors open to light,
enclose the dark.
Between the two
so much they could say.

I go out in sun and rain
and look at open doors,
knowing how they loll their tongues
and barely show their teeth
they search in vain the roofs of their mouths
for something to say.

Would it be the same outside
as in? Does the clamour
of numbers, heart-stopping knocks,
old umbrellas, clobber
and greasy felt hats,
or the towel joyous on its roller,
dampen every word?

Doors are just plain dumb
or their jambs keep them mum,
said an old dog squeezing in
as I come back and drop the catch.
I tell the dog to mind his manners
and go and ask among the overcoats
for news of every room while I was out.

Beneath the brims of trilby hats
lapels have buttoned lips.
There's not a peep from any door,
just jarring notes from every hinge
that make the dog, castrato, sing.

Figure in a Landscape

In the context of his pipe and spittle
he can move mountains

you only have to listen
for the slightly rushed

swallow or the shuffling boot
to know the mountain

was a few feet short
of the twenty thousand

under the volcanic ash
of his pipe

a shift of the eye
gives the game away

but when you are a boy you believe
hills are mountains

The Dog Now Standing

A black blot smudged
from inky stars

weaves through hoary grass
light-sleeking like a midnight locomotive

easing steam from workings
in his fendered brow

a flaring tender
catching in the portholes

of his eyes
legs like spokes

flashing through connecting rods
stopping at every station

Sunday Boy

Such a nice boy on Sundays,
surpliced and cassocked.
Other days likes to make
his presence felt.
A broken fence
says he's been here.
A show-off in the pack
he sneaks up behind
Old Rowbottom with his
daily water bucket
full from the farm thinking
'Nice cup of tea and boiled
turnips' – they're fresh in his
balancing bucket.
SPLASH. Like a severed head
a turnip plummets
into the other bucket,
wets Old Rowbottom.
He stumbles on, arthritic,
bronchitic, to his damp hut.
That nice Sunday boy
is first to run away.

Nuptials

Here come the young man and lady,
All about them
Figures singing in a landscape
Under the high church sky,
Their voices swelled with cathedral clarity.
A pink sun snowstorm of blossom
Comes blessing the 'I do' day.
Here the sun,
Here the snow,
Whither goes the blossom?

Ironing

Ironing is full of thoughts.
A slip, a shirt, is like a reverent
laying out of the owner's soul,
folded and put neater
than anything could be in the flesh.

On this week's ironing board,
next to the usual pile awaiting apotheosis,
mother's cotton dress distils
from its smoothed ampleness
a warmed scent of cleanliness,
its flowered pattern lambent
with the spring light
of a grandson's wedding day.

The dress has been returned
from the old people's home,
with other bodily belongings,
in a reeking old suitcase.

The daughter irons
in this afterlife,
pressing in her thoughts.

Old People's Flat

The intimate click
in the wall between us

is the switching on
of her kettle for tea.

A rustle across the wall
is another month

torn from the calendar,
a leaf nearer fall.

We neighbour these high dungeons
creaking our lives away

in mutual reassurance.
Well before winter

she and I will be strangers,
distanced by noise from the widening

of the outer ring road
that will take more and more people

faster and faster past us.

Getting On

'Good for nothing,'
keeps calling himself.
Sits in a corner,
still wears his cap
going on about being past it.
He, once a young buck.
She, a wraith of a girl
when they met,
can't get on
for his being there,
unused to him in the house
days on end,
goes outside,
cleans windows, looking
in on him
through her reflections.

Glass Ball

Marble-small
it comes to light
on a garden spade.
Rubbed clean
reflects
a thousand suns
from tiny surface crazes,
holds me
transfixed
in the cobalt eye
of its universe.

Like quicksilver
it spills through fingers, rolls
all over, slips off tops
and under cookers, shivers
to a standstill in grubby
inaccessibility.

If retrieved
hurries off any spot
you put it on. Will go for good
one day, quick as it came,
and come to light again
by the foot of someone
digging foundations
where this house once stood.

Bed Of Rocks

They lie side by side
either side a chasm

her sheer brooding rocks
his slithering scree

negotiate either face who dares
but for the night they make camp

let their genies rise
above their sleeping lamps

Saint Veronica

Broom and oleander, almond
almost over, everywhere blossom,
festival and journeying; vines' scents
unfurling, like presents being opened.
Among the knick-knacks, tents and jumping-jacks
money slips like water through the fingers
and the air is warmed on smiles and minstrelsy.

But see the thistles and the thorns
between the hyssop and acacias
and the olive groves, and dust
you'd see for miles begins to rise
from stumbling feet among loose stones.
White and red the blossom drips corpuscular.
Men are on their way to die: two
for the usual evil doings, a third
because they have it in for him. Mark
well later their dark shapes
against the reddening sky above Skull Hill.

There have been others before them,
but today is something special. It's the one
that struggles with his cross the most
that's really upset the applecart.
They'll be happier when they've nailed him up.
The soldiers are giving him a going over –
he said he was King, so they put him in purple,
wove a crown from the weeping thorn
and beat it on his head with palms
like those he'd once had strewn before him.
Now the rabble get their chance, the familiar
hangers-on, banging staves and blowing horns,
whooping Hail King! and baring backsides,
hearing their echoes from every wall.

They're still at it as they leave the city gates,
children running wild, caterwauling, skimming stones
and spitting at the women wailing and pleading
for their man of sorrows. Tender hands
catch at the billowing robes of the city rulers,
are bundled away by flashing hooves
and hefty quarters of the horses of the guards.
Appeals of the poor and maimed
who are sweating and coughing to keep up,
are drowned in the din and dust.
All he does is collapse, the weight
of the cross on top of him. Ropes
slither like vipers, sear his flesh.
The executioners snatch them up,
heave and cuff and kick.
A man dodges through the soldiers'
fists and lashing whips, lifts
the cross from his winded body.
Blinded with blood he wants
to get it over with.
A woman, coming through the cram, embraces,
kisses his barked shins, has time
to brace his head, claw off her head-dress
and mop encrusted blood from his eyes and face
before the soldiers seize her, tear
her away, like they've severed many mothers
from their children.

* * *

The spring flowers are over.
With their shopping, wives are resting
in the market shade at the water-seller's stall.
One takes out a ball of cloth,
not to wipe her brow;
just touches it to her lips –
she has begun this tale before,
and how can it not cause eyes to meet
and heads to shake, this piece of woven grime
she lays out across her knee?
She will not wash it by the river
but feels the contours still
in the palm of her hand: the brow,
the bridge of the nose, the silent
movement of his lips, and sees his likeness
in the centre of its creases.

He is crucified. Let him go.
They are as tired of listening
as they are of the rule from Rome. She should
get on with keeping house. Nothing
is getting done at home.
A herd of goats goes trampling by,
boys twirling sticks behind them. The wives
make a move to go. Sitting around
won't do.

Concept Snake

Released from thicket of dreams

specificity breathes
rears head above crag
testing air
wavering

like a liquorice gun against the sky
muzzle firing forked lightning

before lolloping over the edge
dropping zig-zag smooth
into gorges

unclustering
swimming down streams

plumping
in burglar-black hour
on the mind's grass

coiled stole
chilling the spine
slipping from sleeve
through fang of pen

to be
necessity of snake
gathered in the sun
of a sixty-watt lamp

Bighead

He let me know
he'd climbed Alps
and Himalayas,
fought off crocs
and alligators
in their respective
geographic habitats.
He, barely older than my son,
with Hedy Lamarr clinging on,
riding into spectacular sunsets.

How could I say
I was fighting single-handed
on the tilting slopes
of my mind?

The City Of Funicular Fables

The cableways here are spun across the rooftops
- there's a family careering down the ropeway
on their day out to the hanging gardens or – what
day is it? – to their shrink.
You can reach anywhere in the city by ropeway.
You can whizz off to school or work,
go round the neighbours, shop.
All deliveries come rattling along it
and your mail-order goods go back by it.
The wires buzz
and all commerce is conducted along them.
The sky is black with cables
so sometimes citizens don't know whether
it is night or day,
summer or winter.
The city's hero is the rigger.
Every boy dreams of being up there,
a saviour, solving the city's great funicular problems.
He loses himself in his studies of the bits and bobs
of ropes, with their planets of wires
orbiting stars in snowflake galaxy constructions
through which pass the power and the word.
He dreams of being the power and the word.
But most boys end up as greasers
lubricating the wheels of the aerial cars.
The girls, they are becoming riggers now
and more boys start practising early as trapeze artistes
so they can hang out washing and beat carpets
and shout below to the neighbours.
For everyone lives on top of one another
and the most common greeting is the apology.
The word hello has passed from the language.
They cup hands to mouth for a great hollering
of apology, a public confession:
they are sorry for their dust and drips
falling on everyone below.
Then it's carry on as usual:
a steady rain of words and dirt.
The words evaporate from the breath.
The dirt amasses, layer on layer.
Soon nowhere will be left to suspend another cable.
Everyone will adapt to living like moles,
working with elegant breaststroke
beneath the rusting sinews of their glorious past.

Ancestors

They are alive and well.
I know - they creep in

with the night air,
startle me from dreams,

take off with my reason.
They, who fleshed me out,

gave me memory and tissue,
filled me with guilt.

I shoot thoughts like arrows
into their forest,

wing one.
Shot from his tree
he breaks his crashing fall

hooking tail to branches,
saves himself in the nick of time,

wakes me with a jolt.

Flies In Autumn

Through the window
we see them,
flurries of flakes
black in brilliant sun,
too solid for soot,
mesmerising
like snow in mourning,
an airborne biological weapon
or symptom of global warming.

There is no breeze,
they power their own swirls,
alight transformed
on white walls,
jewelled and dancing
in sun upbeat for October.

Yesterday, leaves flung
themselves at us like knives.

Toby

You, just two,
tread on an autumn leaf,
a sycamore bigger than your feet
and hear its dry crunch,
pick it up,
scrunch it in your hand
then let it go
as though you have inadvertently
held tight
an enormous insect that might bite,
and you laugh from your belly
that such things might be,
and you throw leaves over me
and we run here, there,
everywhere, chasing
autumn out of the park.

Sound-Waves For An Artist In Resonance

In the big seashell
of Tate St Ives

A - A - A - A - A

the little girl
from her pushchair
tests hushed white chambers
for their oceanic
response

In A Cornish Cafe

The man in the cafe
has one thousand three hundred cups

hanging from hooks in the ceiling.
There are dolls' cups and cups

big enough for guzunders,
many with floral decoration

or commemorating an historic occasion.
He brings milk in a jug

and a tiny glass dish for the used tea-bag
on a tray no bigger than A4

which makes the tables seem less small.
Out of season his clientele

are ladies whose wardrobe perseveres
through lavender years -

was that Miss Marple visiting,
at the window table?

They arrive out of puff,
or looking wan. Coming from the doctor

some have faced overnight starvation
and undergone checks. Others are fresh

from the hairdresser, so conversation
flits from admiration to commiseration –

even then it is not all bad:
my wife enjoys her bacon bap

and asks the question the cups pose in unison:
What about washing up? A row or section

in rotation, the man in the cafe explains.
Or is it segment? For he is extending

the collection in a semicircle that burgeons
like sunlight emerging from clouds

of steam in the kitchen, and we are cheered
under the apotheosis of bone china.

No Residence

No study for him
to spread himself out in,
someone serving a sandwich and tea.
He writes on his toe-nail,
sometimes several (stanzas up to ten),
hopping along with pen
in one hand, the ball
of his foot in the other,
knee tucked tight
in the cleft of his chin.

When he's sold all the clippings
and bloodied his toes
he'll write on the seat of his pants,
the back of a bus
or inside the tip of his nose.

His life is in tatters,
his heart shattered,
no-one gives a damn.
Evidence abounds
he's down your way
fuckspraying signs and subways,
his ghetto-blaster cracking plaster
inside the houses and shops.

He can write and rant all he wants –
the council puts up the rates
doing away with his words
and art anatomical,
instead of funding a grant
to give him a space
outside M&S
as poet in residence.

In The Blood

Writing their names, I imitate
their signatures.
Trying to understand.

Were they alive now, they would still wonder.
I hear him saying to her – all that part
of rural Staffordshire in his voice:
'Ey should be among beas' an' mekkin' money.
He sucks at his tongue. Ar 'ad me childer
t' work for me. What's 'ey thinkin' on?

I am drawing fish in the circle of light
from the Aladdin lamp, wanting
to be an artist.
                        Yo'll 'aft get that
out o' y' yed. What d'y' want be that for?
Wey'n alwis bin farmers, wey 'an. Both sides.
In the blood. Never bin owt else.
                                    Beyond the fish
tiny squares of the oilcloth's print each enclose
a faded rose, some this way, some that.

Y' mam's towd yer, pictures've gone out.
Nobody nowadays much 'as 'em. Ar know
wey'n got birds' nests an' one o' grapes upstairs
an' one Mam cut off th' calendar
o' women gleanin'. But wey're owd fashioned.

He blames the grammar school.
                                    Yo've bint' that school
an' y' know nowt. But y' mam let y' go.
Dun y' know,
                I know very well, father.
Ar was 'elpin' me dad soon as Ar could walk, nearly.
An' left school when Ar was 12.

The tiny squares of roses go
in all directions. But mainly towards
those big hands at the top of the table.

Yo'll clem if yo' dunna get down
to some proper work. Th'is no money
in bein' a artist. An' wey'n 'aft pay
f'th' learnin'.
                        How pleasing the curve
of this fish as it changes direction.

Morning. Wet. The house smells of the yard
and breakfast. Liver, bacon. The edges
of yesterday's mashed potatoes crisping
in a dish on the range. Spoonfuls
of bacon fat.
                        'Ey wunna get this
once 'ey leaves wom.
                        I sit in my absence.
Suddenly, I'm present.
                        Yo'
mun 'elp me muck out, after.

Market day. Slapping of sticks on flanks.
Men, overalls slimed khaki, move beasts about
in sale rings littered with straw.
He waits for his stock to come up.
                        Nare
'ey comes up wi' PILOT. Aeroplanes.
Rushes out every time one goes o'er. Knows
'em all. Germans an' all.
                        Around him
others affirm it's unimaginable.
They aar in agreement and call him 'Boss'.

Well, he's unarguable with.
                                    PILOT!
Ar anna 'avin' that. Anyroad, Arsh'
think war'll be o'er by time 'ey's owd enough.
Ar dunna know what wey'll mek on 'im. Ar
thote 'ey'd come round, but 'ey anna.
                                         His stock
are next.
                    Next best 'ud 'a' bin a job wi'
th' auctioneers. Office job. But 'ey'd
'a' bin among stock 'ere – 'ere a' mine!
– in Utcheter Smithfield.
Under the hammer
his stock do well. Elated. Confounded:
                                         But
'ey'll 'ave nowt at all to do wi' farmin'.
It'll 'aft' be aeroplanes. Where the' mek 'em.
Factory job. 'Ey wunna stand that. 'Ey'll
be back soon enough. What the' put in 'is yed
at that school, Ar dunna know.

His signature.
Spikey Victorian slopes
from what schooling he had.
On pink cheques. Forms
from The Ministry of Agriculture and Fisheries.
But not one of consent for an offspring
to join up.

Hers.
Done with her pinky finger held proud,
steadying the soft shapes of her letters. Not in full.
Just 'Mum', enquiring
why I haven't been in touch.

Gut Need

From my gut I tell you it was no trouble.

Witness the selection of keen knives
kept in a canvas roll
for killing the family pig.
                          Old thing,
taken to like a puppy, then grew
bristle on back and ears I could
get my nails into, scratching
in mutual satisfaction. Not just
when we shared with you what we'd had
on our own plates – we'd come and see you
between times, easy in thought
and exchange our sweet-sour breaths
and guttural gratitude. Not sparing a sigh
for your predecessor sustaining us still
from her mouldering hangings wintering
and summering in the fly-quiet attic,
and daily look into those blonde lashes flickering
in contentment that we should tend you so well.

Doctor Shipman, you and I have the belly
for this need: to kill and cure.
Such benevolence filtered through your beard
they thought it Christmas, those old ladies.
Am I less two-faced? Were you any worse
following up your emptied syringe
with sympathy cards? How many? More
reprints than enough in the end?
For what it's worth you never charged
in with a killing team, turned
on your quarry, lashed her
squealing to an oak bench, medieval thick,
stirred out the clots as you watched
her life drain into an old work-bucket
to make black puddings, blew up
her bladder for sport –
          as far as I know.
Yet I blench as I feel our shoulders touch.

The Day I Killed My Father

The day I killed my father
was like any other. He was
really getting on my nerves.
I can't remember what about
but there we were having lunch,
which we called dinner. At least
they were, my mother and big sister.
He was in a spindly old chair
with sunken upholstery and terrible
unsteady legs for someone his size.
I was rampaging about
and they'd got fed up with me playing
with my food. I started shaking
my father's chair. He laughed
and was enjoying the rocking motion,
when things changed.
The chair tipped over sideways
and smashed on the flagged floor
with him in it and knives and forks
flying. His dinner only just missed me
as I jumped out of the way.
My mother and sister said,
Now you've done it. He's dead.

Hope Farm, Nineteen-Forties

Above the house a thrush
sings hope at dusk.
Inside, a lamp is being lit.

Across the yard the cattle
have been looked and settle
in their stalls. Their heat
seeps to the stars
like toast through cracks in doors
and web-frothed window panes.

Over a rosary of black-edged finger nails
my father's lips move in whispers
in the kitchen, recapping jobs
in the daily husbandry of beasts
as he scrubs and towels each finger.

Minding not to shatter
the mantle's filament
as chimney glass and globe
are lowered over flame,
my mother's mallow hands are steady.
Her breasts, pinnied
in floral print in daytime
smell of eggs still hot from the hen;
at night of the charred wick
and paraffin shedding light
on the weekly paper's oily print
and wedding photographs
of those who my father says
have gone daft this week.

We lean towards the light
to sew, or darn a sock bulged
on a wooden mushroom, or play
snap, or ha'penny nap, strip
Jack naked. Or ludo with counters
the colours of rationed confectionery.
The youngest listens to his crayons'
swish across a Woolworths' wood-pulp pad,
drawing shoals of fish till suppertime.

A Boy And Three Clocks

My mother,
winding the big clock,

remembers something like yesterday
that happened years ago,

says: Time goes on wheels.
I, not big enough to know better,

imagine clockwork
turning large in thoughtspace.

My sister's bedside clock is oiled
by the aroma of medication she needs

to ease her breathing.
Her blunt-nailed fingers pump

the glass spray's rubber bulb
the way she milks cows.

On winter days my parents
leave their cavernous old bed smell

before dawn, like they once
went out fighting mammoth.

Alarmed by their luminous black clock
barking out its innards,

they go swinging lanterns
like fireflies about the yard.

The Day I Saw A Fly, 1942

The day I saw a fly
in my father's beer
he stood talking
to a friend
in our November kitchen's
drear and couldn't see
the waving fly
drowning in his glass.
They wondered how the war
would end and pondered
on the sorry state
of humankind,
not to mention kids.
Through the bottom
of his glass I watched
despairs of fly and father
meet in his moustache
until one disappeared.

Homework In Ink, 1944

A pungency that sits
in the nostrils still.

Ink. Blue as window light
through a poison bottle.

Sweated over in can't-do
homeworks wandering

into a no-man's land
of nine o'clock nights

beyond suppertimes.
Labouring with dip pen

in the circle of light
from the Aladdin lamp,

its mantle shushing
over the table's oilcloth.

The squeak of the nib's point
bottomed in the bottle

by blue fingers,
natty at that age

but all thumbs at this game.
Mother struggling to help,

Father: I left school at 12,
snoozing. The hollow steel heart

that is the nib
catching its point,

splitting and stalling,
bleeding in the blinding

snow of the paper. Knowing
the answer stares you in the face

with the spatter of blots.

1943

My father,
following his May morning shadow
in through the door,

is lifted, having observed
the call of the first cuckoo
with spit and coin.

A birdnester himself
he swivels four eggs,
speckled and turquoise,

still warm,
in the cup of his palm.
Blackie's, he says.

Under the basting pan
the coals in the grate
blow banshees of flame.

My mother
wills tiny yolks into pearls,
turns them out on my plate.

Sunday Afternoons

We roamed like hunter-gatherers
Sunday afternoons,
Fred, me, Froggy and the Evacuee.
Digging pignuts, picking nuts and berries,
whittling sticks for spears
and budding mountaineers.
Fred, me, Froggy and the Evacuee

up for all seasons.
Stumbling up to our thighs
in drifts of brittle snow.

Chewing spring leaves
we called 'bread and cheese'
from rows of burgeoning hawthorn.
Catching newts and tiddlers,
our arms wreathed in duckweed.

Fred, me, Froggy and the Evacuee
lying on our backs
crushing forests of summer grass,
squinnying through the dazzle
of our virgin minds.

Boomeranging conkers and chestnuts
with bent sticks. Knowing which hips
to eat, which
to put down backs to make them itch.
Fred, me, Froggy and the Evacuee

misjudging the fading light –

the chaos of late again for tea,
the curse of irregular verbs,
unfinished essays on Laissez Faire,
quadratics that won' t work out.
Fred, me, Froggy and the Evacuee
packing books into satchels
that reeked of spilt milk
and Monday mornings.

The Archway

They went up
in the afternoon
with pitchforks
and lanterns
held like shields,

crept, while the bats slept,
into the big loft
above the archway
where the house shook hands
with the cowshed.

'What use such creatures
worrying night air?' the farmer
and his labourers said. 'You never know
what they might do to the corn
or the milk.'

The air is thick
with ammoniacal stink.
'Tanner I'll get most!' one man grins.
'I'll double that,' the farmer says.

Like shirt-sleeved remnants
of an army with pitchforks for pikes
they pin bat after bat against rafter.
Fork clashes with fork, jabbing
at the flurry of wings,
bringing them fluttering down
in a crimson drizzle,
for crushing under studded boot.

In an hour the men have cleared up,
shovelled bats into buckets,
deep-buried them in the manure heap
and gone for their tea.

The Farmer's Daughter

Her clogs clatter across
the flagged kitchen floor

still wet from her mopping.
She takes the four-ten

from its leaningplace
by the blackleaded range,

becomes a murderous silhouette
passing through the door,

squirts the blackbird with shot
on the strawberry bed

and the rooks when they've resettled
in the old yew.

Another day it's the pigeons
on the corn and the magpie

killed like a heretic cleric.
She is purging the land

the way her heavy-handed father
has taught her.

Another day a neighbour,
disturbed in the early hours

by noises downstairs,
rises to fall from the blast

of his own twelve-bore
in the hands of a disquieted son.

Winter

He wants to stuff
the east wind,
go out, feed stock
like he's always done,
the hay blowing about him,
mud sucking the soles of his boots.

Indoors,
still wears his cap
like a talisman
warding off draughts
that howl round corners,
splitting his bones.

The wood in the grate
sputters. He recognises
the cut of it. Off
the old ash he felled
a summer ago.

Blue Slop

His old coat is on the door.
Blue slop he called it, a lightweight

worn every summer.
Pockets sagged from spanners,

staples, old nails and the hammer
that looked like him

saved keep walking
to and from the barrow

that carried its own load:
the big oak-headed mall,

rolls of barbed wire, posts
he'd cut sharp in a haze of smoke

from the coughing black engine
that drove the circular saw.

It's on the door
and I can talk to it

as though he's still in it,
shaped as it is to his bent arms

and hunched back,
smelling of his iron and earth.

There's probably still a toffee
melted in its wrapper,

or a peppermint worn thin
in the rust dust and fluff

of a pocket. Like the cough-drop
he'd defluff and hand to me

after I'd levered the awkward-jawed
pincers round a post

to tighten the wire
he'd pluck and tune.

I'll pass that one up,
leave it for him, wherever he is.

His Boots

His everyday boots
steel-studded and skiddy

in the early morning yard
were moulded to his feet.

Weathered to dulled shine
they lasted for years

through cuckoo-spit Aprils
and stubbly Septembers

and daily sloppings of sheds
in the hoof-pocked yard.

His mushroom-darned socks
burnished the boots' insides

like copper kettles
that sang across the kitchen years

after age and east winds
seized his joints

confined him
to the pallor of inactivity.

Now those boots are soggy
and covered in moss,

his daughter has filled them with flowers
and strung them from branches

like aeolian harps
in the weed-tangled air.

Market Day

Picking up your watch from a drawer
I'm caught in a memory of you
in what you called your market best
with this silver watch and chain on show,
its dangling key so small for your large hands
you might have let me wind it.
Instead you had me blacking your boots
and leggings and reeking of Cherry Blossom
so you'd swagger among your peers
following the auctioneer from ring to ring,
tipping your tongue to your stub of indelible lead
from your waistcoat pocket to note
what store and fatstock made.
That tongue freed up in the smoke
of the market bars and massaged
with peppermints before you came home.
Appearances mattered. You'd rail against drink
and 'Smoking will burn holes in your pocket!'
still rings in my ears. I tried both
without much pleasure of decadence,
only nausea in my eagerness
to go against you. Through my reflection
in your watch glass I see the broken fingers
tumble around the pointless hours
and remember how I tilted tiny balls
into place in a child's puzzle.

E.

(1917-1992)

Asthma shut down her lung forest,
blew out her oxygen for schooling.
Instead she learnt at home
to grow things, even on bad days
be useful around the place.

She grows flowers
that spring hot as torches,
wave in the breeze like night processions.
Captures them like royalty on Kodachrome.
She is good with a gun.

Her thoughts, a thatch of things
rough-edged as crows' nests,
come out in caws and gasps:
blackbirds are rifling her raspberries,
currants and cherries.

She comes out, sullen in floral pinny,
swings up her four-ten
(kept in a gap by the chimney breast) –
I awake with a start: a loud bang
splits open my dream-head darkness

and I remember her
picking up the bird by a foot
and going back to making cakes,
the sound of birdsong returning.

Lost Touch

As fresh-faced kids
we picked up anything.
Apples with blemishes
we said had canker,
when your mother
was dying of cancer.

The college the village
was famous for
left around
old rugby balls
we thought were flawed
because they were not round.
So it was OK to take them.

Your father was one of us,
he picked up an old bus,
chocked it up on bricks,
never used it for chickens.
Just let us have it
as the hub
of all our games.

For ten years and more
we never saw each other
after leaving school.
I went away, you stayed
on your father's farm.
Then, one day, with wife and daughter
I dropped in on you, from the city
as you must have seen it.
Your father sat by the same old fireplace.
You came in, it might have been from harrowing,
and you and I stood tongue-tied
in the middle of the room
as rough and smooth hands touched.
Your sister, who was always
party to our games,
came in
and wondered
who the townies were.

Evening Cocktail

The thrush
is a repeater
repeating
down
corridors
of years

one once was the only sound
on a winter evening
when I sat growing up
in my mother's house
oblivious to the smells
of earth through flagged floors
bacon curing in salted thrawls
the steel tang of scoured pails
the family's overalls and damp coats
hanging in the wooden porch

one is singing now
through the gloom of a January evening
repeating
repeating
that cocktail of smells
so pungent

thrawls: a colloquialism (probably local) for the
large stone or ceramic sinks in which the butchered
pig parts were laid and salted.

Then

nights were for sleeping

now
comfort coincides
with pain

 right side
is middling except
left
nostril
packs
in

 supine i'm a
cracked violin
                strings overtight
curling
toes
to
chin

 left
side
lets
pit-
    props
             cave
               in
my heart a squashed plum

 prone   head in the pillow
so
alone

 before bones
told me their ways
before skin said thin
a bone
in
the
leg
said
bone
idle

The Kiter

Up here
the wind is planing
the greenness,
fine-combing the autumn grass.
As a boy
with wind-burned ears
I'd see how far I could lean
without falling
on my face.
Now I'm grizzled
and stragglier
it's the one sport I can do better.
In my old coat
I'm like a bat –
you'll see me in gateways,
bodykiting
in funnels of air,
mittened hands out flat,
thumbs wedging on my hat,
the wind
in my clothes
like I could say something
important
to the people down there
valleywise.
Somebody should listen
to an old kiter
having fun on the hills –
there might be something in it
instead of camouflaging your knees
in front of the fire.
Here I am
at thirty degrees to the normal,
manhandling the wind,
a Cnut of the air,
a commander of ground forces,
when you all said
a puff of wind
would blow me down.

Postcard

Why
when we are getting on fine
do you go?
Is it the leaves
that fall about you?
Or the snow?
Autumn
I told you
has to come and go.
Spring will ever promise
and end on a low.
Please send address
and let me know.

Biographical note

Bill Mycock was born at Lower Loxley, near Uttoxeter,
Staffordshire, in 1934. He was educated at Bradley Street
School, Uttoxeter; Denstone village school, and Alleyne's
Grammar School, Uttoxeter. Instead of farming, the occupation
of all his male and most of his female relatives, he took up
aeronautical engineering. He later worked in industrial
journalism and photography as an information officer and editor
for an international group of engineering companies. He and his
wife live at St Agnes in Cornwall. They have a daughter and a
son.